Folkestone
in old picture postcards

Martin Easdown and Linda Sage

eb

European Library ZALTBOMMEL / THE NETHERLANDS

Acknowledgements

We would sincerely like to record our thanks and appreciation to the following for their encouragement and assistance with illustrations and sources of information used in the compilation of this book: Alan F. Taylor, Peter and Anne Bamford, J. Salmon, Rob Illingworth and his staff at Folkestone Library's Heritage Room, Peter and Sally Russell, Ray Clare, Tom and Bethany Easdown and particularly Eamonn Rooney for kindly reading and checking the proof.

Bibliography of reference sources used

Bishop, C.H., *Some Folkestone Worthies* n/d

Bishop, C.H., *Folkestone: Story of a Town* 1973

Easdown, Martin and Eamonn Rooney, *Tales from the Tap Room* 2000

Easdown, Martin and Linda Sage, *Folkestone under Water* 2001

Easdown, Martin and Linda Sage, *Rain, Wreck & Ruin* 1997

Easdown, Martin, *A Grand Old Lady* 1996

Easdown, Martin, *Victoria's Golden Pier* 1998

Hart, Brian, *Folkestone's Cliff Lifts* 1985

Hendy, John, *Folkestone-Boulogne* 1987

Paine, J.M. and K.S., *The History of the Grand Hotel, Folkestone* 1994

Rooney, Eamonn D. Alan F. Taylor and Charles E. Whitney, *Folkestone in Old Photographs* 1990

Taylor, Alan F., *Folkestone Past and Present* 2002

Whitney, Charles, *Folkestone: A Pictorial History* 1986

BACK IN TIME

European Library

post office box 49

NL – 5300 AA Zaltbommel/The Netherlands

telephone: 0031 418 513144

fax: 0031 418 515515

e-mail: publisher@eurobib.nl

www.europeanlibrary.com

Introduction

Folkestone — ferries, fish and finery someone once said. Well for the time being the ferries have gone and the fishermen are not as plentiful as they used to be, but happily Folkestone still exudes some of the elegance that once made it the most fashionable seaside resort in England. The world-famous Leas is a delightful cliff top promenade with views of France on a clear day, while a stroll around the tree-lined avenues and crescents of the West End will flashback the town's refined past. The arrival of the railway in 1843 had prompted the growth of Folkestone and its emergence as a select watering place, yet of course the history of the town goes back a lot further than the Victorian era.

In Roman Britain Folkestone appears to have been a settlement of some importance as indicated by the discovery of a substantial villa on the East Cliff in 1924. During succeeding invasions by Anglo-Saxon tribes, Kent was mainly settled by the Jutes and one of their burial grounds from about the year 600 was uncovered close to Dover Hill on the outskirts of the town in 1907. In 630 King Eadbald of Kent established a priory on the West Cliff for his devout Christian daughter Eanswythe. The building was soon lost to cliff erosion, but a Benedictine Priory founded in 1095 survived until Henry VIII dissolved it in 1535. Out of the priory grew the establishment of the Parish Church of St. Mary and St. Eanswythe in 1138, which due to the ravages of the French in 1216 had to be rebuilt between the 13th and 15th centuries. Further work had to be carried out during the 19th century after its western end had fallen down in 1705 and in 1885 the relics of St. Eanswythe were rediscovered in the Sanctuary.

During the Middle Ages Folkestone was a fairly prosperous community engaged in fishing, farming and quarrying. The first market had been granted in 1205 and in 1313 the town was granted a Charter of Incorporation by Edward II allowing it to elect a mayor, bailiff and 12 jurats. By this time Folkestone was a Corporate Limb of the Cinque Port of Dover and suffered an attack by the French and Scots in 1378. Henry VIII visited the town in 1543 in connection with the laying out of a harbour, yet no work was carried out and it was not until the reign of Charles I (1625-1649) that a primitive seaport was first established. However, successive attempts during the 18th century to improve the harbour were to be wrecked by ferocious storms.

In 1697 Jacob des Bouverie became Lord of the Manor, which from 1765 also included the title of Earl of Radnor with the eldest son becoming Viscount Folkestone until ascending to the earldom.

Later Earls were to radically change the face of Folkestone, but for now it was still a small fishing town with a profitable line in smuggling. The 'Pelter' brig was beached at the Warren as a headquarters for preventive officers, yet such measures hardly proved to be a deterrent and on 26th May 1820 a mob from Folkestone broke into Dover Gaol and rescued 11 of their compatriots who had been caught smuggling. The Folkestone fishermen also showed they were just as wise to the notorious Press Gangs; they sent their wives over to Holland to give birth, so any sons threatened in the future could claim Dutch citizenship!

Plans for an improved port were conceived in 1804 when Lord Radnor petitioned Parliament for the construction of a stone harbour, and in 1807 an act was passed authorising the Folkestone Harbour Company to start work. The foundation stone was laid in 1808 and three stone jetties were eventually built; though that was not to be the end of the story.

Seaside resorts began to take off following the publication in 1750 of Dr. Richard Russell's treatise on the benefits of bathing in and drinking seawater; nevertheless, until after the coming of the railway Folkestone was to remain an insignificant watering place. 'Two elegant bathing machines for the recreation of gentlemen and ladies' were in place by 1797, yet two of the town's earliest attractions, the Chalybeate Spring at Foord and the Cherry Garden, were both well away from the seafront. Laying below the hills a couple of miles north of Folkestone, the Cherry Garden in particular was a popular summer resort from 1750 where military bands played amongst the cherry trees, a cottage sold refreshments and a natural lake was a feature. In the town itself, the New Theatre (or Folkestone Theatre) was advertised in 1774 as being situated in a small building on the Bayle, which later became the Harveian Institute. It was described as a tarred weatherboarded structure with a roof like an upturned boat, back-less benches in the pit, two boxes near the stage and a gallery. Three other attractions of the early seaside were medicinal baths, assembly rooms and circulating libraries. Indoor baths allowed their patrons to reap the health-giving benefits of sea water in comfort without venturing into a freezing sea and in the early 19th century Messrs. Gill, Elgar and Wills all operated baths in Folkestone. The Apollo Assembly Rooms could offer balls, card games and billiard tables and the main circulating library was in the High Street where Messrs. Purday (1791-

1806), Roden (1806-1811) and Tiffen (1811-??) were successive proprietors. A guidebook of 1810 neatly sums up the attractions of Folkestone at this time: *The amusements of this place are but few when compared to some of its neighbours. There is however a small theatre, which is occupied in the winter, and an assembly room called the Apollo. The circulating library, kept by Roden, however may be considered one of the principal amusements. The library is regularly furnished with the London and Provincial newspapers, magazines and other periodical publications, and it is well supplied with new books. And this repository forms a most agreeable lounge every Tuesday and Friday evening during the season and is well attended.*

In 1825 the Earl of Radnor took the first serious step in creating the future resort by making available building plots with long leases. Few were taken up because as yet Folkestone had not the potential to realise a substantial investment. As Pigot's Directory says in 1840, when the population of the town was around 4,400: *As yet there is a lack of lodging houses as compared to the demand, but great facility is afforded for the erection of new ones. A large extent of land, mostly eligibly situate, has been laid out by the Earl of Radnor for building purposes, and there are few places, it is presumed, that would better repay a well-directed building speculation.*

By now there were serious problems with the harbour silting up and in 1842 the Folkestone Harbour Company went bankrupt and the Government put the harbour up for sale. However, in the same year navvies were hard at work in Folkestone on the South Eastern Railway's (SER) line from London to Dover and the town was about to undergo a dramatic transformation.

1. The SER was opened in Folkestone on 28th June 1843 with a temporary station in the vicinity of the present Folkestone Central Station. SER Chief Engineer William Cubitt designed the splendid 19-arch brick viaduct across the Foord Valley, depicted here shortly after opening looking west along what became Foord Road. This viaduct was completed by the autumn of 1843 allowing a permanent station to be opened on 18th December 1843, which became known as Folkestone Junction. In February 1844 a line was opened from the Junction Station down to the harbour to enable coal to be transported up to the coking ovens at the station. Folkestone Central Station was opened as Cheriton Arch on 1st September 1884 to forestall a plan by the London, Chatham and Dover Railway to open a branch to Folkestone through the Alkham Valley. The name of the station was altered to Radnor Park in September 1886 and then Folkestone Central on 1st June 1895. On the outskirts of town Shorncliffe Station was opened on 1st November 1863 and was renamed Folkestone West on 10th September 1962. At the same time the old Junction Station became Folkestone East but it was closed on 6th September 1965. The harbour branch, one of the steepest on the railway system, currently remains in limbo with no boat trains to serve.

HARBOUR AND PIER FOLKESTONE

2. Meanwhile the SER, in dispute with Dover Harbour Board over the siting of the railway terminus there, acquired the dilapidated Folkestone Harbour for £18,000 and opened a cross-channel service to Boulogne on 1st August 1843. An extension of the harbour branch, complete with swing bridge, was opened across the harbour in 1849 allowing boat trains to terminate at a new station. Further expansion occurred when the Customs House (seen in the centre of this postcard by Shoesmith & Etheridge from the 1920s) was added in 1854 and a new low water pier was built in 1861 to handle the larger steamers that had previously encountered tidal problems at Folkestone. The railway was extended onto it in 1876, and the harbour arm was to be lengthened again in 1883 and between 1897 and 1905. As well as the cross-channel service the harbour boasted a considerable trade in coal, timber and ice up to the 1920s, which was transported in vessels chiefly owned by local businessmen. The first cars were craned on and off the ferries in 1911, but it was not until 1st July 1972 that a car link span for roll-on roll-off ferries was introduced at a cost of £1m complete with new terminal and customs buildings. However, Sealink ended the link with Boulogne on 31st December 1991 and though Hoverspeed introduced a seacat service on 11th April 1992, this too was discontinued in 2001 leaving Folkestone without a ferry link to the continent.

3. To complement its new cross-channel service, the SER asked William Cubitt to design a hotel to be placed by the Inner Harbour. The Pavilion Hotel was opened in 1844 and this view shows it about 1884 after it had been extended in the 1860s (when it passed into private hands) and just prior to a winter garden being added in 1885. J.B. Edwards took over the hotel in 1882 and had it entirely refaced in red brick and terracotta in 1889. In 1896 the hotel changed hands again, to Henry, Frederick & Co who extended it in 1898-1889 to accommodate 300 bedrooms (a view of the updated hotel can be seen in photograph 56). By this time the hotel had gained a Royal prefix and was to remain fairly successful up to the Second World War, though its huge size was beginning to count against it. At the end of the war the Royal Pavilion never reopened and in 1960 was acquired by M. Burstin for £70,000 to provide accommodation for elderly people. The grounds were utilised for the new Hotel Burstin in 1974-1975 and the Royal Pavilion itself was largely demolished in 1979-1980 to make way for an extension to the Burstin, which nevertheless continues to use the west wing of the old hotel.

4. With the arrival of the railway and cross-channel link, the Earl of Radnor concluded the time was now ripe for the development of a select watering place on the lines conceived by James Burton at St. Leonards in Sussex and in 1845 engaged noted London architect Sydney Smirke. He drew up a plan for the stately Wear Bay Estate on the East Cliff complete with interconnecting glass passageways leading to an aquarium and reading rooms, but nothing was built save for the Radnor Bridge that linked the East Cliff to the town. Smirke's next project was the creation of Tontine Street as a high-class development of Regency-style shops. Work began in 1848, but was only half completed when it became obvious Folkestone was not yet ready for such improvement. However, by 1885, when this photograph was taken, the street had become the town's main shopping area. The funding of the project was on the tontine principle by which subscribers each receive an annuity during his life that increases as their numbers are diminished by death. The Folkestone Improvement Act of 1855, building upon the founding of gas (1842) and water (1848) companies, stimulated further development by laying out a system for main drainage.

ALBION VILLAS FOLKESTONE

5. The 1840s also saw the earliest development of the West Cliff with the erection of Nos. 1 and 2 Priors Lees in 1846 by R.W. Boarer, and Albion Villas, which is pictured here on this postcard from about 1906. Albion Villas consisted of three pairs of stuccoed houses and were later joined by the terrace on the right, christened Priory Gardens. Between July and September 1855 Charles Dickens stayed in No. 3 Albion Villas (behind the lady with the parasol) and wrote part of 'Little Dorrit' in the house, which is commemorated by a blue plaque on the wall. Dickens affectionately described Folkestone as 'Pavilionstone' in the article 'Out of Town' for 'Household Words', a weekly publication of which he was editor. Despite the hot day, everyone in the photograph is well covered up, for suntans were frowned upon before the 1920s. The horse carriage, bath chair and goat cart stands were situated here and help make this a typical Edwardian scene. The ornamental fountain on the left was unveiled in memory of philanthropist Sydney Cooper Weston in February 1898. It was later removed to the East Cliff in 1921, where it still stands.

6. The greensward on the edge of the West Cliff was known as the Leas (the original spelling was Lees), a Kentish dialect word meaning a common or open space of pasture. A path had run along the cliff for many years, but from the 1850s the Leas began to be developed as an exclusive 1½-mile promenade and select hotels and residences were erected, including the Langhorne as seen on this 1904 postcard. The bandstand was added in 1895, and Lord Radnor's policeman patrolled to ensure all 'undesirables' were kept off in a bid to maintain the area's social exclusivity. By 1900 the Leas was acknowledged as one of the country's finest cliff-top promenades by the wealthy, who strolled along in their ceremonial dress (especially during Church Parade on a Sunday morning) to partake of the air and the stunning views of the English Channel and France; sometimes with their nannies and maids in tow. A contemporary article commented: *Folkestone since it became a watering place has always retained a hold on the more moneyed of those who go to the sea in the summer. It does not lay itself out to attract the ephemeral tripper, thus on the Leas one may see the distinguished and wealthy rub shoulders in pleasant contiguity, instinct with the satisfactory knowledge they have achieved their weekly devotions and that a good dinner awaits a good appetite.*

7. In conjunction with the expansion of the Leas, the land lying behind it on the West Cliff was to be urbanised throughout the second half of the 19th century with broad avenues, crescents and squares containing elegant stucco and red brick residences. Castle Hill Avenue, seen here on a postcard by Upton Series in the 1930s, was one of the showpiece thoroughfares complete with dual carriageway separated by a tree-lined boulevard. On the right of the picture can be seen the Hotel Continental Wampach, opened as a high-class hostelry by Charles Constant Wampach in 1886. By 1909, the hotel had been extended to hold 80 bedrooms along with six suites of private rooms, state rooms and a large dining room. At the rear of the hotel was the Elite Tea Gardens where Mr. George Cooper and his Parisian Quartette played daily. During the First World War the Wampach was used by the army and upon its reopening in 1920 the name was briefly changed to the Excelsior. By then, however, the golden days of Folkestone's grand hotels were on the wane, though the Wampach struggled on until the early 1970s. In 1974 the empty building was badly damaged by fire and was eventually demolished in 1982-1983 to make way for the Court Place retirement flats.

8. One of the earliest of the select hotels in the West End was the West Cliff, opened in 1857 by Thomas Masters in what had been four separate houses. In 1860 the hotel was sold to a speculative company 'The Folkestone West Cliff Hotel Company Ltd', who raised £60,000 in capital by selling £1 shares. An additional wing was opened in the same year to provide a ballroom, which became particularly admired, while promenade concerts on the rear lawn were another feature. Further refurbishments were carried out in 1898 and this postcard by Harmer of Sandgate in 1910 shows the West Cliff at its height of popularity. During the First World War it was used as a Canadian Eye and Ear Hospital and upon its reopening as a hotel was renamed the Majestic. Yet, as was the case with all of Folkestone's big hotels, things were never quite the same again after the Great War and in 1962 the Majestic was closed and quickly demolished to make way for a row of shops and maisonettes known as Majestic Parade.

9. Old and new Folkestone are seen together about 1870 with the recently built Town Hall in the background and the old coaching inn the Kings Arms, complete with horse coach. Since the arrival of the railway in 1843 the coaches had largely been pushed out and only a few remained to provide a service along the coast to Dover and Hythe and inland to Canterbury. The days of the Kings Arms, which dated back to 1692, were numbered and it was eventually closed on 18th December 1881. The Town Hall had been opened on the site of the Cistern House (used as a town hall from 1830) on 15th June 1861; designed by Joseph Messenger, a porch was later added in 1879. After over a century of service it was put up for auction in 1986 and in the following year the ground floor became Superdrug (Waterstones from 1997). In 1990 the Silver Screen cinema was opened on the upper floor.

10. Improvement of the seafront, where a regatta had lately been inaugurated, was also taking place on the beach to the west of the harbour. This photograph from circa 1869 shows the four typical Victorian stucco terraces that make up Marine Terrace, laid out in 1859-1860, and on the left Marine Crescent nearing completion. This had been built on the site of the town's first gasworks, opened in 1842 and moved to a far more suitable inland site in 1866. On the right of the photograph can be seen the distinctive Venetian-style outline of the South Eastern Railway's harbour office. The 'Clock House', as it was known, opened in 1844, but was later demolished in 1899 to make way for an extension to the Royal Pavilion Hotel.

S 5391   **THE LIFTS AND BATHS, FOLKESTONE.**

11. Just to the west of Marine Crescent, the Bathing Establishment was opened on 20th July 1869 and is pictured here about 1905 on a postcard by Kingsway Real Photo Series. Designed by local architect Joseph Gardner in an attractive Italianate style the many attractions on offer included hot and cold sea water baths, medicated baths, vapour baths, a swimming pool, billiard, reading and refreshment rooms and a large saloon with balcony. An extension was added at the front in 1888 to accommodate a larger swimming pool, though it was eventually covered over and used as a dance floor. Later known as the Marina, falling attendance's led to closure in 1958 save for the smaller swimming pool, which under the guidance of former cross-channel swimmer Sam Rockett was used by local schoolchildren. Unfortunately over the following eight years the building became increasingly derelict and was demolished in 1966. Subsequent proposals to develop the site have never materialised and it remains an under-used car park.

1035. THE LIFTS, FOLKESTONE.

12. To ease the connection between the Leas and the bathing beach a water-balance tramway, similar to the three already in use at Scarborough (and the one at Saltburn-by-the-Sea), was opened by the Folkestone Lift Company on 16th September 1885 at a cost of £3,224. Supplied by R. Waygood & Co. of London, the two cars ran a distance of 164 feet on a 5' 10' gauge track and could carry up to 15 people each. The method of operation was both simple and ingenious: a strong steel cable connected both cars, which had water tanks under their bodies. When the tank of the car at the top of the lift was filled with water the weight sent it down the cliff and hauled the other car up. The lift proved to be so popular, an adjoining funicular was opened in 1890. This had a steeper incline (leading to tiered seating in the cars, for 16 people each) on a track of 155 feet and can be seen in operation on this postcard from the 1920s by Wiseman Homer. However, declining passenger numbers led to the closure of the 1890 lift in 1967, though happily the original 1885 structure survives in the hands of Shepway District Council and is the second oldest water-balance tramway in the country (one year younger than Saltburn).

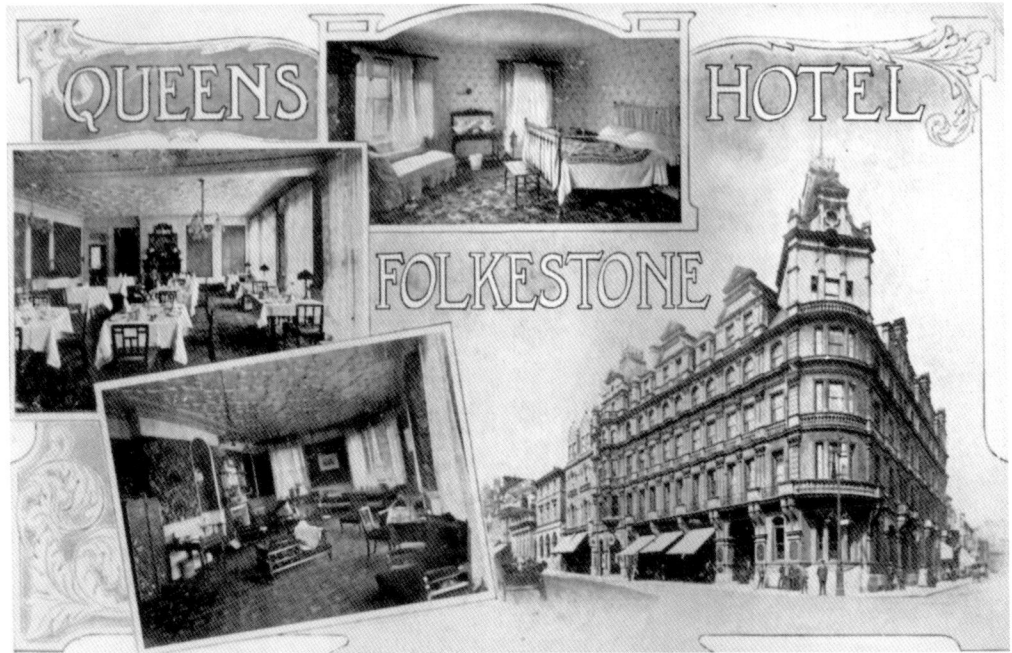

13. Away from the West End developments were also carried out in the older parts of Folkestone and by 1881 the town's population had risen to 18,822. The Queens Hotel, seen here in four vignettes on a postcard from about 1906, was opened on 18th January 1885 at a cost of £30,000 on the site of the old Kings Arms (see photograph 9). Nonetheless this imposing Victorian building struggled financially in its early years by failing to attract substantial numbers of high-class patrons; probably due to its rather noisy town centre location opposite the Town Hall. No dividends were paid to shareholders and part of the building was let to a firm of bankers for seven years. A new restaurant bar (1893) and electric lift (1896) were added, yet the hotel continued to struggle and in 1903 the Queens Hotel Company was wound up; its assets being acquired by the Folkestone Hotels Syndicate for £16,000. They managed to make more a go of the hotel and the Bodega Bar was to become popular with both businessmen and locals. Sadly in 1962 the Queens was sold for redevelopment and was pulled down the following year to make way for a typically insipid 1960s creation known as Queens House.

Winter Garden, Royal Pavilion Hotel, Folkestone

14. The year 1885 also saw the assembly of this winter garden in the grounds of the Royal Pavilion Hotel, seen here in the 1920s. The typical iron and glass conservatory building was erected by John Weeks & Co of Chelsea and was officially opened on 21st March 1885. Its original use as an elegant lounge with light orchestral music was altered to a dance hall after the First World War, but expensive maintenance costs led to the building's demolition. The Town Council had rejected an earlier proposal in 1879 for a huge winter garden on Lower Sandgate Road. Such schemes were all the rage at the time with their theatres, lounges, aquaria, skating rinks and covered promenades all under one roof, yet huge financial costs led to most of them never getting off the drawing board. Of the few that did, only the example at Blackpool still survives. The smaller iron and glass winter gardens as at Folkestone were more affordable, yet the only free standing Victorian example you will find at the seaside today is at Great Yarmouth.

15. A rare photograph of the winter garden-like Arts and Treasurers Exhibition building under construction in 1885. Situated in Bouverie Road West, Folkestone's own Crystal Palace was opened on 15th May 1886 at a cost of £16,000 to house high quality art and antique items from around the world, which could be viewed to the accompaniment of a string orchestra. A special railway line was laid from Shorncliffe Station to serve the exhibition and with Folkestone receiving ever-increasing numbers of wealthy visitors there were high hopes for its success. Unfortunately it appears Folkestone's other attractions held greater interest and visitors to the exhibition were few and far between. After only five months the promoters gave up the ghost and cleared the building of its treasures. The obscure rail connection was torn up and the building lay unused until The Folkestone Pleasure Gardens Company acquired it in October 1887 for only £2,100. Work was quickly put in hand to prepare a temporary theatre in time for Christmas 1887.

16. A full reconstruction of the Pleasure Gardens Theatre was carried out during the winter of 1890-1891 to allow a full view of an enlarged stage with a new semi-circular gallery. Between February and April 1896 ten boxes and a dress circle were added to make room for 300 extra people. The original glass roof was also covered over for the comfort of patrons (the building had suffered from being too hot in summer and too cold in winter). This postcard shows the theatre in 1906 when it was being visited by many of the leading operatic and dramatic companies. In 1913 the foyer was converted into a concert hall and an annexe housed a gymnasium, which also doubled as badminton courts. Sixteen acres of grounds provided tennis courts, croquet lawns and a show ground, popular for military tournaments and displays. Illuminated evening concerts were also a feature and during the winter months a roller skating rink was provided. Regrettably, falling attendances led to the cessation of live entertainment in 1956 and from November 1956 to May 1964 the building was used as a cinema before it was demolished to make way for an office complex that is now the town's police station. The post office seen in the picture still functions over the road from the former theatre.

17. Every self-respecting Victorian seaside resort harboured ambitions to build a showpiece pleasure pier and after initial opposition from the Town Council, Folkestone was to acquire the Victoria Pier. It is seen here on a lantern slide shortly after it was officially opened by Viscountess Folkestone on 21st June 1888. Promoted by the Folkestone Pier & Lift Company, the 683-foot-long pier was designed by Noel Ridley and erected by Heenan & Froude of Manchester, who six years later were involved in the construction of Blackpool Tower. The floating landing stage seen at the end of the pier was opened in 1889, but was rarely used by pleasure steamers and was dismantled around 1903. The Pier Pavilion could seat up to 1,000 people and initially housed high-class concerts, operatic overtures and chamber orchestras, yet the pier rarely paid its way and in 1907 it was leased to local entrepreneur Robert Forsyth. Discarding the old entertainments, he quickly introduced more popular attractions such as wrestling, novelty shows and the world's first international beauty contest (contestants were shipped over from Boulogne!). The Olympia Skating Rink was added at the pier entrance in 1910 and a popular feature for many years was diver Lawson Smith. The end of the pier came during the Second World War, when firstly it was sectioned as a defence measure and then largely destroyed by fire on Whit Sunday 1945. The remains were removed between 1952 and 1954.

SWITCH BACK RAILWAY. FOLKESTONE. P.H.47

18. One of the great mysteries of 'Fashionable Folkestone' was why Lord Radnor gave permission for this switchback ride, usually associated with working class resorts, to be erected on the beach in his select watering place. Patented by the American La Marcus Thompson in 1884, Thompson's Patent Gravity Switchback made its first appearance in England the following year and in Folkestone on Friday 17th August 1888 with free rides for the first hour. The wooden structure ran parallel to the promenade up to 40 feet high and customers sat on a small trolley, which was pushed along the undulating course to the far end. Then the assistants pushed it around the bend before sending you back on your way along the return section to the start point. The switchback was loved and loathed in equal measure: Folkestone Town Council was firmly in latter camp (saying the ride lowered the tone of the resort) and tried to have it removed; yet many of Edwardian High Society (such as Prime Minister Herbert Asquith) greatly enjoyed the experience. Unfortunately, the positioning of the switchback led it to suffer repeated damage by stormy seas and following neglect in the First World War the ride was dismantled.

19. You can almost feel the cold yourself looking at this view of a frozen sea-closeup front during the winter of 1889. Photographed from the newly-built Victoria Pier, rows of bathing machines can be seen on the beach (along with the horses that pulled them – it was said the colder the sea, the more beneficial the bathing!) as can the original version of Fagg's Bathing Carriage. On the left is the clubhouse of Folkestone Rowing Club, erected in 1884 at a cost of £300, who hosted the annual regatta. The circular building on the beach by the clubhouse is a camera obscura, a popular attraction of the Victorian seaside. Inside was a rotating periscope head containing a mirror and lens, or curved prism, which projected an image onto a dish-shaped screen giving a panoramic view of the world outside. The final camera obscura was removed from the beach in 1936, while the clubhouse was dismantled following the rowing club's relocation to Sandgate in 1946.

20. Folkestone's development as a choice seaside resort was further enhanced in 1892 with the opening of the Marine Gardens. The bandstand, shown on this postcard from 1904, was added in 1893 and was the town's first, though it was also the earliest to be demolished, in 1927. Pierrots and concert parties performed in the gardens, as did the Folkestone Amusements Association bands under Messrs. Prickett and Stratford and the Folkestone Town Band, while just out of sight on the left was a rather ornate toilet block and shelter with a flat roof used as a viewing platform. In 1926 part of the gardens made way for the new Marine Gardens Pavilion and the remainder later disappeared under an extension to the Rotunda Amusement Park. In the background can be seen Marine Crescent, now due to be refurbished following years of neglect.

Sandgate.

The Hill Lift.

21. Following the success of the Leas Lifts, the Sandgate Hill Lift Company was formed to provide a lift from the extreme western end of the Leas down to Sandgate Hill, where a horse tram could then be caught to Hythe. Like the Leas Lifts, the design of the buildings was placed in the hands of prolific local architect Reginald Pope (assisted by C.E. Robinson), with Waygood once again supplying the lift equipment. The 5' 6' gauge track ran for 670 feet and crossed Radnor Cliff Crescent by way of a bridge, but due to the changes of gradient from 1 in 4.75 to 1 in 7.04 the cars had to be independently operated with a brakeman on board. The lift was officially opened on 20th February 1893 and this postcard by the Victoria Series shows it about 1904. However, following a satisfactory beginning, the lift became unprofitable and was closed in July 1918, the Lift Company being finally wound up in 1924. The lower station seen here still survives, though in a much-altered state, as Croft House. Behind the lift can be seen Spade House, built for novelist H.G. Wells in 1901 and now a nursing home.

22. The Earl of Radnor, who himself had a residence (the Manor House) erected on the Leas in 1896, provided a suitably genteel attraction on the cliff-top promenade in 1894 with the opening of the Leas Shelter. Designed by Bromley & Cowell and set into the cliff face by local builders Hayward & Paramour, the shelter consisted of a central hall 62 x 31 feet, where a light orchestra or band performed daily, and the canopied balcony seen here where splendid views of the English Channel could be obtained. The building was leased to the Folkestone Amusements Association, formed in 1893, and three of their attendants can be seen, along with some early deckchairs first introduced on to the Leas in 1881. Also worthy of note are the splendid wrought iron brackets supporting the canopy and the hanging flower baskets. The shelter was closed in 1925 and dismantled to make way for the new Leas Cliff Hall.

Upper Leas Bandstand & Hotel Metropole, Folkestone. No.146.

23. To cater for the ever-increasing numbers of affluent visitors to Folkestone, the western end of the Leas was provided with two of the large imposing hotels that were becoming very popular in the stylish resorts by the 1890s. The first to be built, and seen here on a postcard by H.B's F & L in 1910, was the Metropole Hotel on a former polo field. The Folkestone Metropole Hotel Co. Ltd promoted the hotel and Messrs. Jennings & Co started work in 1895 to the designs of James D'Oyley of London. The attractive red brick and terracotta building was opened on 1st July 1897 by Gordon Hotels at a cost of £160,000 and contained 250 bedrooms, ballroom, dining room, library, drawing and billiard rooms and a grand hall foyer. The bandstand was originally sited in the rear grounds of the Metropole, but was moved onto the Leas in 1902 following complaints from the hotel's guests over the noise; it became little used by the 1930s and was demolished in 1948. The hotel itself suffered in comparison with its competitors because it only opened for the summer season and in 1928 was offered to Folkestone Town Council, who politely said no. Eventually the Metropole was closed in April 1959 and now consists of flats, and arts and fitness centres.

THE GRAND, FOLKESTONE.
LOOKING SOUTH OVER LEAS, PROMENADE AND SEA.

24. The Grand Hotel joined the Metropole at the western end of the Leas in 1903 and is pictured on this postcard of circa 1905 complete with tariff. Local builder Daniel Baker conceived the hotel as a high-class establishment: work began on 28th March 1899 and it was officially opened as the Grand Mansions on 12th September 1903. The Grand also boasted a good-looking red brick and terracotta exterior, clad around a steel and reinforced concrete frame, along with a glass conservatory at the front of the building. Amongst the many facilities the hotel could offer were music rooms, lounges, billiard rooms, garage and hairdressing salon. King Edward VII was a regular visitor due to the fact he personally knew both Mr. Gelardi, the manager from 1903 till 1943, and Head Chef Mr. Dutru, formerly of the Savoy Hotel, London. However, until a licence was gained in 1920 all alcoholic drinks had to be sent out for. Having been acquired by Kensington Hotels in 1947 and then by Associated Hotels in 1961 the Grand maintained its popularity until the late 1960s, but as the hotel trade crashed in Folkestone the building was stripped and threatened with demolition in 1973-1974. Fortunately this was never carried out and in 1975 the Grand was acquired by Michael Stainer, who has carried out an ongoing sympathetic restoration scheme using items that once belonged to the hotel or are period pieces. Part of the building was reopened as a hotel, though it also houses 67 self-contained flats as well as a very popular monthly antiques fair, for which the plush interior of this fine building is just the right setting. Indeed, the Edwardian ambience of the Grand has led it to be much in demand as a filming location.

THE GRAND, FOLKESTONE.
THE TERRACE, OVERLOOKING THE LEAS, PROMENADE, AND SEA.

25. The glass conservatory at the front of the Grand Hotel is seen here to good effect on a postcard from the same series as the previous illustration. The conservatory was a typical elegant Edwardian palm court with its wicker furniture and large potted ferns. It was known by one and all as the 'Monkey House' on account of the large numbers of spectators who peered inside to see if they could spot any of the hotel's numerous eminent and moneyed guests. Their arrival in the town had been heralded in the Weekly Visitors List (class also came into effect in the local directories, which divided the residents into 'Court' and 'General'). The most desirable 'spot' of all was Edward VII, who in 1909 opened the hotel's new sprung floor ballroom and then had the first dance on it with the Queen, followed by a second with his companion Mrs. Alice Keppel. The King and Queen also presented medals to staff to commemorate the event. The King's association with the Grand is maintained by the location of a restaurant called Keppels in the fully restored Monkey House.

26. The next addition to the list of Folkestone's attractions was the Leas Pavilion, opened on 1st July 1902 opposite the Leas Lifts and seen here shortly afterwards on a postcard by E. Bumpus Pain, whose shop can be seen in the picture. Architect Reginald Pope had got around the 'Ancient Lights' clause the adjoining properties enjoyed (which meant no building could be erected that blocked their light) by placing the structure below ground level. Finished in attractive buff terracotta with art nouveau windows, the Leas Pavilion was originally a high-class tea room 'securing the best class of visitors only' to enjoy the ladies light orchestra. However, in 1906 a small stage was added and concert parties such as the 'Gypsies' were engaged. In 1928 a full size stage and rows of seating were introduced and the Leas Pavilion was converted into a theatre. The following year saw Arthur Brough (of 'Are You Being Served' fame) acquire the lease and he was to present over a thousand productions at the theatre for the next forty years. Sadly falling attendances throughout the 1970s and 1980s meant the theatre could not survive and it was closed in 1985 following a production of 'An Unexpected Guest' by Agatha Christie. Fortunately the building was preserved and converted into the Leas Club with bar, bowling alley and pool and snooker tables.

27. The western end of the Leas acquired its own lift on 31st March 1904 with the opening of the Metropole, or West Leas, Lift by the Metropole Lift Company. The 5' 6' track ran 96 feet down the cliff face from opposite the Metropole and Grand Hotels to the Lower Sandgate Road where the attractive red brick entrance building, designed by Reginald Pope, can be seen on this Edwardian postcard view by English Series. As was the case with the Leas and Sandgate Hill Lifts, resident engineer John Collins oversaw the operation of the Metropole Lift. During the Second World War the lift was closed and fell into disrepair, and was subsequently never reopened. The operating company went into liquidation in June 1951 and the lift was dismantled, leaving little trace of its existence. Many of Folkestone's wealthier visitors of course never ventured beyond the comparatively safe and exclusive upper class haven of the Leas. As one contemporary account says: *Folkestone holds itself aloof from the sea, caters for a class that does not sit on the beach, a class that it confers on personages both estimable and ennuyant.*

Lower Sandgate Road, Folkestone

28. However, for those who did partake of a ride on the Metropole Lift down to the Lower Sandgate Road, the pleasures of wooded walks fanned by fresh sea breezes awaited them. The Lower Sandgate Road had been opened as a toll road by the Earl of Radnor in 1828 and was developed as an under-cliff garden from 1876. This photograph of about 1890 shows the tollhouse, which, though no longer functioning as such, still displayed until recently a board showing the various levels of charges. The pine walks of the cliff were said to be especially beneficial to the health of invalids; a big selling point prior to the First World War when many people came to the coast for the benefit of their health. In the last few years the section of the road beyond the tollhouse looking towards the pier has been radically altered with the opening of the Lower Leas Coastal Park.

29. The surviving parts of old Folkestone close to the parish church also held an attraction for the visitor. The Bayle, taken from the Norman word 'bailey' meaning a castle yard, not only once housed a castle, but also a battery and St. Eanswythe's Priory. King Eadbald of Kent founded the priory in the year 630 for his devout 16-year-old daughter Eanswythe, who died ten years later and was subsequently canonised. The original building was destroyed by cliff erosion and later versions suffered at the hands of the Danes in 867 and Earl Godwin in 1052 before a Benedictine Priory was established by the Lord of the Manor Nigel de Muneville in 1095. This survived until 1535, when Henry VIII dissolved it and the stone was used to build Sandgate Castle. The British Lion pub, pictured in this c.1910 photograph, may have originally been known as the Priory Arms from 1460 and stands beside the priory site. There was also once a Norman castle in the area (possibly on the site of an earlier Roman fortification) and in 1560 a defensive battery was founded, which in 1862 became the principal station of the Royal Artillery Coastal Brigade. However, it was closed in 1888, though the Battery Commanders House, complete with gunpowder store, still stands.

FOLKESTONE – High Street

30. The narrow and distinctive (Old) High Street connects the Bayle and parish church to the fishmarket and harbour. Seen here on this postcard from about 1903, it contained a number of buildings dating back to at least the 17th century. Charles Dickens liked to stroll up and down the hilly byway during his 1855 stay in Folkestone and described it in a letter to Wilkie Collins: *I went out after dinner to buy some nails and I stopped in the rain, about halfway down a steep, crooked street, like a crippled ladder, to look at a little coach makers house where there had just been a sale.* Fortunately the High Street largely escaped bomb damage in the Second World War (unlike its 'twin' Dover Street, later rebuilt as Harbour Way) and looks much the same today as in this view. One of its most interesting shops is Rowlands Rock Shop where you can still see this most traditional of seaside confectionery being made.

31. The bustling fishmarket held a particular fascination for the more cosmopolitan and daring visitor who tended to romanticise about the life of a fisherman. This postcard from 1906 shows a fairly busy scene on the Fishermen's Stade, erected by the SER in 1860, probably at the weekend, judging by the amount of children there are about. Nets can be seen drying, while the large fish shed, erected in 1863 and one of three, is where the captured fish were sorted, gutted and sold. The tramlines led to the SER workshops, transferred to Dover in 1922. Around this time there were about fifty fishing boats operating from Folkestone, but declining fish stocks and EU regulations have shrunk this number to approximately ten now, employing thirty people.

Wreck of the "Good Intent" Folkestone.
WEDNESDAY, OCT. 5TH, 1904.

32. The life of a fisherman was often anything but romantic however, as emphasised by this rare postcard from 1904. The sudden appearance of a strong south-westerly gale during the evening of Wednesday 5th October 1904 caught a number of fishing vessels off Folkestone unawares and they were soon battling through waves of immense proportions in their frantic bid to the reach the sanctuary of Folkestone Harbour. One of the vessels to find itself in peril was the Folkestone fishing smack 'Good Intent' (FE21), returning from fishing off Hythe with three members of the Saunders family on board. The boat was still afloat, but it was heading dangerously towards the treacherous rocks of Copt Point. The stricken crew fired distress flares, which were seen ashore by a large crowd gathered on the Stade, yet the launch of the Folkestone Lifeboat 'Leslie' was delayed when it kept being swept back onto the beach by the huge waves. Eventually however, a successful rescue was duly carried out, though, as this postcard shows, the Good Intent was dashed upon the Copt Point rocks and was a total loss.

Ship's boat
driven on rocks
7 men drowned

Hole in ship's side

S.S. Shelder Stroom in collision and aground at Folkestone
7 men drowned - December 8th 1907.
Photo Polden + Hogben, Folkestone

33. Three years after the wreck of the Good Intent, the Dutch steamer *Scheldestroom* also foundered off Folkestone, as documented on this postcard by Polden & Hogben. The *Scheldestroom* had been making her way down the Channel on the stormy night of 8th December 1907 when she was hit on her starboard side by the schooner *Forfarshire*. The impact of the collision knocked out the steamer's engines and the captain ordered the ship's lifeboat to be lowered. He jumped into the craft first followed by twelve of his crew, but unfortunately it capsized and a desperate struggle for life ensued. Two of the crew were hauled back aboard the ship, while four managed to swim ashore at Folkestone, yet sadly the captain and six of his crew were drowned. The remainder of the crew left aboard the storm-battered *Scheldestroom* resolutely stayed put until they were eventually coaxed to board the Folkestone Lifeboat *Leslie* after an attempt to tow the vessel to Folkestone failed. A second attempt by two tugs was later successful. A sad fact of this tragic story is if all the crew had stayed aboard the stricken ship, no lives would have been lost.

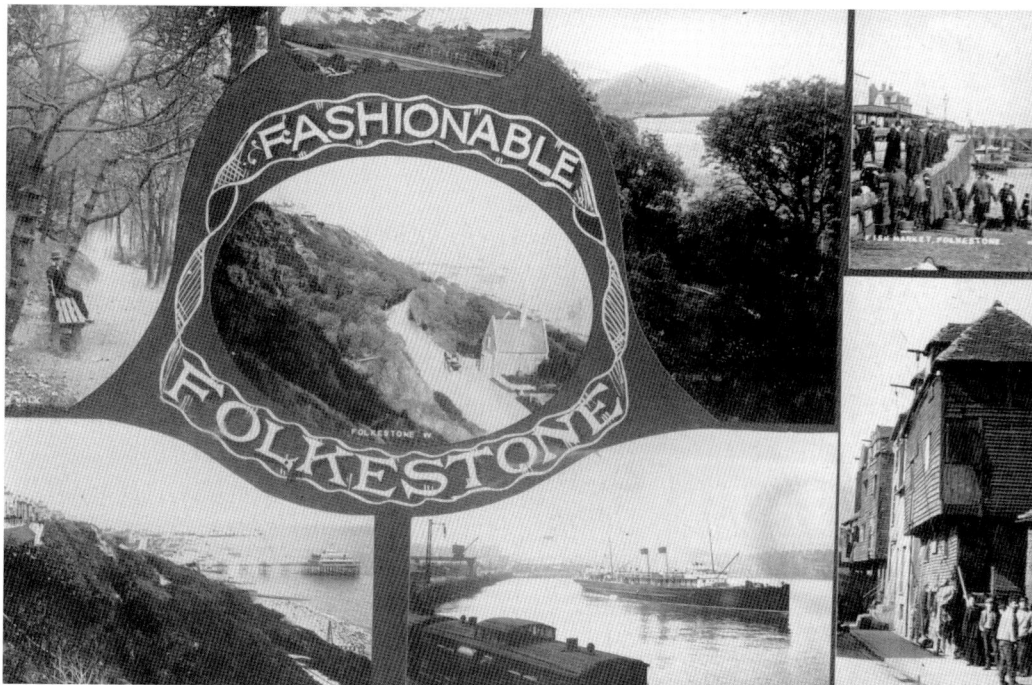

34. 'Fashionable Folkestone', as it was termed, was at its height in 1907 when this multi-view postcard was produced showing some of the attractions the town had to offer. A visitor at the time enthused: *I have visited all the watering places in the British Isles and find none with a seafront surpassing Folkestone. Its noble residences facing the sea with the lovely grass promenade of the Leas before them, the Madeira Walk so sheltered and the Lower Sandgate Road with its gardens and shrubbery ending in the magnificent beach with its rows of colourful bathing tents. Excellent bands, morning, afternoon and evening, play on the Leas, the fashionable rendezvous of the town, while on wet mornings you can sit in the Leas Shelter, a spacious concert hall in the face of the cliff, and while listening to the band discourse sweet music, you have the panorama of the English Channel. The Leas Pavilion dispenses a delightful afternoon tea to the sounds of a ladies string orchestra and the Pleasure Gardens Theatre has over 18 acres of grounds and attractions. Then there is the Warren, that romantic spot of which Folkesto-nians are very proud and which they call 'Little Switzerland'.*

35. Orchestral music was the soundtrack of Fashionable Folkestone and Herr Moritz Würm and his bands were a great favourite in the town between 1895 and 1914. Herr Würm, an accomplished violinist, was a native of Lemberg in Austria (now the Russian city of Lvov) and looks typically Germanic with his upturned moustache and medal-strewn uniform on this postcard by Lambert Weston. He was managed by the Keith Prowse organisation that arranged for him to appear at the more select resorts where orchestral music was likely to be more appreciated. As well as Folkestone, these included Eastbourne, Bexhill and Cromer (for the opening of the pier in 1901). Between 1903 and 1906 Herr Würm and his Blue Viennese Band performed two concerts daily in the Victoria Pier Pavilion during July and August, while his Red Viennese Band played under the awning on the pier head in the morning and in the pier gardens while afternoon teas were served. Amongst the other venues in the town where Herr Würm appeared was the Leas Bandstand; though for a period from 1905 Sunday concerts were banned in Folkestone altogether, as it was felt this day of worship should not be defaced by such frivolity. Street entertainers, such as hurdy-gurdy men, had already been banned from 1900 for not being in keeping with the tone of the resort. Herr Würm's musical repertoire was wide-ranging and included waltzes and quadrilles, marches and gallops, intermezzos and ballet music, varied with violin, trumpet and bassoon solos. However, at the outbreak of the First World War Würm left quickly for America, anticipating enemy 'aliens' would be interred.

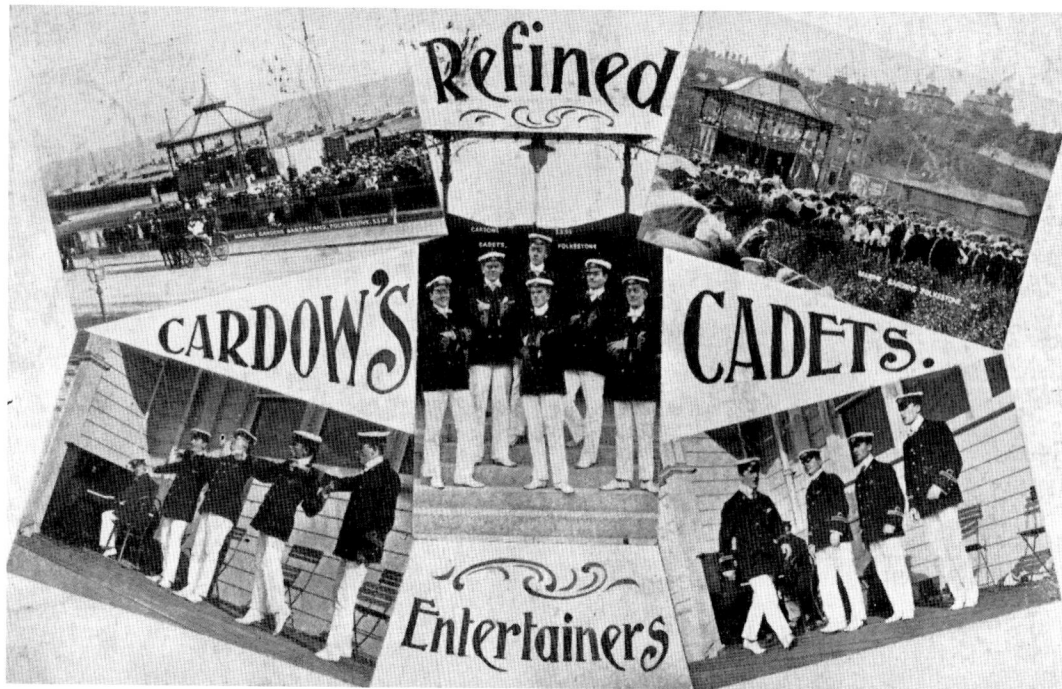

36. For those who found Herr Würm's orchestral music perhaps a little stuffy, there was always the more down-to-earth variety act of song and comedy as performed by Cardow's Cadets, a long-time Folkestone favourite for over twenty years. Led by Charlie Cardow, the troupe can be seen on this vignette postcard from 1905 appearing at the Marine Gardens Bandstand. They could also be found on a wooden stage in the grounds of the Bathing Establishment, which became the Red Roof Chalet, where they were resident until at least the late 1920s. The sailor suits seen here were the troupe's usual garb, though they sometimes appeared in Pierrot costume. After the First World War, by when women were part of the act, they were usually turned out in smart suits and dresses. Cardow's Cadets could be found performing at other resorts, yet they were always at their most popular in Folkestone.

37. A Pierrot troupe (perhaps Cardow's Cadets) in Marine Gardens are captured on this postcard by the West End Photo Co. in 1907. A sign on the stage says seat prices range from 1-3d, but most of the crowd were prepared to stand for free! The Pierrots tried to get round this by asking the best looking of the troupe to go amongst the crowd with a bottle in order to get a few pennies off the ladies at least; this was known as 'bottling'. The appearance of Pierrots in Marine Gardens reveals that by the mid-Edwardian period Folkestone was becoming a resort with two faces. Exclusivity still reigned up on the Leas and in the West End (where Pierrots were definitely out of bounds), yet the seafront was beginning to cater more to the middle and working classes. Pierrots had been introduced into England in 1891 and performed a mixture of song, comedy, mime and magic. Their distinctive clown-like costumes were very much a feature of the English seaside during the Edwardian period, but they were to be supplanted by concert parties after the First World War.

38. A typical Edwardian beach scene with children playing in the sand at low tide is captured by Clark, a local photographer, in 1908. In the background can be seen the second version of Fagg's bathing carriages that we saw in photograph 19. These unique pair of structures (one each for men and women) ran along a railed track into the sea, thus overcoming the problems of beach gradient and eliminating the strain associated with the moving of the standard bathing carriages. They were patented by Walter Fagg, manager of the Bathing Establishment in 1887, and this improved design appeared two years later, with a further refinement being carried out in 1895. The carriages housed the changing compartments and a corridor led to a safety cage in the sea for non-swimmers, while diving boards were available for the more adventurous. At the end of the swim each compartment housed a wash basin and fresh towels to clean off the saline particles. These distinctly superior bathing machines remained popular with Folkestone's well-to-do visitors for a number of years, but by 1910 mixed bathing was in full swing further west along the beach and patronage had seriously declined. By the time Mr. Fagg had passed away in 1914, the track had been removed and the carriages had been fixed onto the beach.

39. The exclusive Fagg's bathing carriages were too expensive for most people's pockets and as undressing on the beach was strictly forbidden, the alternative was to use a bathing machine or tent. The bathing machine had been pioneered at Scarborough in the 1730s and Folkestone possessed two by 1787. However, due to the steep shingle beach, they were unsuited to Folkestone and were rarely used after 1900. Up until then the sexes had been strictly segregated for bathing, but following the construction from 1906 of a new promenade along the western half of the beach, a mixed bathing ground was established there. A large changing pavilion was erected and gaily-coloured tents lined the beach. This postcard from 1909 shows bathers using a pleasure boat landing stage to enter the sea from the main beach, where bathers were still segregated. The four gentlemen appear to be ensuring the sexes are kept well apart as the ladies are all in the foreground and the gentlemen in the background.

40. Despite being an attractive place in which to live and visit, Folkestone, like anywhere else, suffered its fair share of natural and man-made disasters, as shown on this 1908 postcard. The perils of early motoring are revealed for all to see as a car hangs precariously over the cliff on the Slope Road during the afternoon of Wednesday 6th May 1908. The vehicle, a Mercedes belonging to a Mr. Cohen of Park Lane, London, spluttered to a halt going up the hill and swerved back into the railings, which gave way. Fortunately the car grounded on its gearbox, which prevented it falling down the cliff, though its back end was left hanging over the edge. During the next couple of hours the stricken car became the centre of attention until it was finally pulled back onto the road with the aid of ropes. An examination of the vehicle at the Pavilion Garage found it had sustained surprisingly little damage and Mr. Cohen was soon able to continue on his journey to London.

41. A Christmas card-type postcard scene of the parish church and West Terrace covered in snow during the harsh winter of 1908-1909. The Folkestone Herald rather delightfully set the scene by reporting: *The earlier falls having cleared the air, the snow was of an unusual whiteness, and scenes in the town as the sun sparkled on the snow-clad world were strikingly beautiful. Folkestone for a few hours might have claimed also the title of 'Our Lady of the Snows'.* However, it must not be forgotten the difficulties a heavy fall of snow can bring. Workers had to battle through waist-high drifts to get to work and road traffic was paralysed, though local schoolchildren enjoyed having two days off school and no doubt put the snow to good use! Folkestone Corporation rounded up five hundred men and twenty-three horse and carts to clear the main roads and paths.

42. This dramatic postcard, used just a few days after the event, shows George Mence Smith's oil and colour merchants shop well and truly ablaze during the afternoon of Monday 26th April 1909. This 'Afternoon of Cracking Entertainment' was conceived by a plumber carelessly leaving his blowpipe alight amongst the highly inflammable contents of the shop and before long this exciting drama was in full swing. As the smoke from the conflagration poured into the sky a huge crowd gathered to watch the main act involving sixteen firemen hurling water onto the burning building from all directions. Shops in the constricted High Street were closed and boarded up, as it was feared rivers of oil aflame would run down the ancient thoroughfare. However, splendid work by the firemen prevented the fire spreading in that direction, though adjoining properties in Bayle Street were damaged. Fortunately the only fatality proved to be the shop cat, which died from smoke inhalation.

43. The aftermath of the Great Flood of 29th October 1909 is captured on this postcard view by Polden & Hogben showing a wrecked wall of the North Board School (now Mundella) in Black Bull Road. Fast flowing torrents of water fed by torrential rain had rushed down from the hillside above and swept through the school before cascading down the hill into the Foord Valley. The water gathered in a whirlpool at the junction of Black Bull Road and Foord Road outside the public baths, where, fed by the overflowing Pent Stream that had burst its banks, it reached a height of over eight feet. The nearby Red Cow public house was badly damaged as was Fowler's builders yard next door, yet no lives were lost in the flood and by next morning the water had largely gone. Unfortunately, this was not to be a one-off occurrence and there have been several repeats since, most notably on 12th August 1996.

44. 'The Fall of the Giant' is splendidly captured on this postcard by the local West End Photo Co. The incident took place on Saturday, 4th March 1911 when a steamroller ran dangerously out of control down Sandgate Road before crashing into the front of the East Kent Arms. Folkestone Corporation had hired the engine from their counterparts in Hythe to assist with road repairs in Church Street, but as it began to descend the lower half of Sandgate Road the brute assumed a mind of its own and ran uncontrollably down the hill scattering everyone in its path. The runaway looked set to plunge headlong into the Town Hall until it swung round outside the pub, causing a wheel to come off and strike the outside of the building. Like some stricken monster the machine collapsed onto the pavement, breaking the back axle and dislodging the boiler, which was holed, allowing steam to escape with a great roar. Luckily no one was injured and later that day men from Messrs. Aveling & Porter of Rochester arrived to remove the engine.

45. Just three months after the steam roller drama in Sandgate Road occurred this traction engine smash out at Stelling Minnis on 3rd June 1911, this time sadly with fatal results. The engine, belonging to local firm Arnold & Son and with four men aboard, was pulling three trucks along Hatch Lane when the driver miscalculated the edge of the road, causing the vehicle to topple over a bank and overturn. The steersman, David Botting, was killed instantly, but the driver, Edward Bailey, was rescued by the two other men, Stephen Palmer and William Beer, and taken in a serious condition to the Royal Victoria Hospital. He held on to life for another week before unfortunately succumbing to blood poisoning.

46. The other side of the Fashionable Folkestone coin was the poverty that lurked in the eastern areas of the town, and in 1913 the Town Council declared that many houses in the fishmarket and Dover Street/Fenchurch Street areas were unfit for human habitation. This photograph from 1894, however, shows a slum that had already been swept away, the notorious Narrows, off Harvey Street. In the fishmarket area, Radnor Street, East Street, The Stade and three alleys – Clouts, Dunns and Bates – were all scheduled for demolition, yet it was to be another twenty years before any action was carried out. Meanwhile the tremendous growth of Folkestone during the late Victorian and Edwardian periods (the population had jumped up to 33,502 by 1911) led to the need for greater artisan housing and rows of solid unpretentious terraces sprung up in Foord and around the roads to Dover and Canterbury.

47. A splendid Edwardian photograph of a Fishermen's Band dressed in all kinds of interesting costumes, probably for some special occasion. A Fishermen's Fife and Drum Band was known to be in existence by 1856, but it was disbanded and not reformed until later in the century. Sister Katherine, a nurse attached to the fishermen's church St. Peter's, encouraged this new band and allowed them to practice in her cottage on the Stade. Hopefully for the neighbours they did not have a big bass drum as seen in the photograph!

48. Another celebratory gathering in the fishing quarter, this time at the top of North Street. The exact reason of the festivity is unknown, though it is probably to do with the coronation of King George V in 1911 or a peace celebration in 1919 following the ending of the First World War. Some of the participants appear to be in fancy dress; notice the cowboy outfit, sailor suits and gentleman dressed as a teacher. North Street was originally known as New Island and most of its houses dated from the 18th century; unfortunately they were nearly all pulled down following the Second World War after suffering damage from enemy action. The only survivor was the Lifeboat Inn, seen in the background, which opened as a public house in 1861 and continues to function as such today.

49. Close to the Inner Harbour, Beach Street was an interesting area of pubs and cafés that was to be sadly destroyed by enemy action in the Second World War. One of its casualties was Walter Tame's refreshment and coffee house at 11 Beach Street, which was flattened by a parachute mine on 11th November 1940, killing Mr. Tame, his business partner Charles Rainsford and their wives. This photograph dates from about 1908, just six months or so after the restaurant was opened in the former Queens Head public house. The pub, which dated back to at least 1861 (though the building was much older), was closed by the licensing authorities on 28th December 1907 and Walter Tame had been its licensee for the last twenty years. He was allowed to remain in the building after closure by brewers Nalder & Collyer to run his new café and in 1920 acquired the premises outright for £700. By the time of their demise Walter Tame and 11 Beach Street had been associated with each other for over fifty years.

50. Like all large towns during the Victorian and Edwardian periods, Folkestone bristled with numerous public houses: in 1903 for example there were 140 alcohol licences issued. Twenty-six of these were situated in the crowded area around the harbour and fishmarket, but during the nationwide purging of public houses between 1903 and 1914 a number of the more disreputable premises were closed. One of those that escaped the axe was the well-run South Foreland at 4 Seagate Street, pictured on this rare photograph from about 1910. The South Foreland was in existence from at least 1824 and had been in the hands of the Jordan family since 1862. Harry Jordan, who was at the helm at the time of this picture, was licensee from 1883 until 1913. Indeed the pub, which was regarded as one of the better hostelries in the area, and was sometimes even frequented by the 'toffs' of the West End, remained in the hands of the Jordan's until it was completely destroyed by a German parachute mine on 11th November 1940. All that remained was the cellar, which was fenced off and colonised by Buddleia until covered over by a car park in the 1950s.

51. Another Folkestone public house, the Red Cow, is pictured just before the First World War with licensee George Summerfield on the right. Mr. Summerfield was landlord between 1912 and 1917, having previously been at the Royal Standard for twenty years. The Red Cow was situated in the former spa village of Foord that had long been swallowed up by residential Folkestone, and was the lodging house for the few visitors who came to taste the chalybeate water. The pub dated back to 1682 and the original building still survives behind the Victorian brick frontage, which was added by brewers Alfred Leney of Dover in the 1880s. In spite of a few troubles over the years, including serious flooding by the nearby Pent Stream and bomb damage during two world wars, the Red Cow remains open and has had its bar area recently extended with the addition of a conservatory.

52. Returning to the seafront, this most unusual postcard shows a view of a lady skater and her instructor (on the right) skating along the deck of the Victoria Pier in 1909. What with the uneven planks and the gaps between them it must have been a bit of a hair-raising experience! Roller-skating had first taken off in the mid-1870s, but then waned in popularity before a second craze exploded in 1908. Robert Forsyth, the enterprising manager of the pier, took advantage of this by providing a temporary rink in the Pier Pavilion during the winter of 1908-1909. Having proved its popularity, the rink was to remain in situ until May 1909, when the pavilion had to be prepared for the summer season.

53. The success of the temporary skating rink on the pier led Robert Forsyth to construct this permanent rink in the gardens to the west of the pier entrance. Local builders Messrs. Daniel Baker & Co began work during the winter of 1909-1910 to a design by Reginald Pope and the Victoria Pier Olympia Skating Rink was opened to the public at Whitsun 1910. The rink measured 160 x 72 feet and the entrance fee of 1s included hire of skates and tuition from a team of seven smartly attired instructors (who ensured customers only skated anti-clockwise). As can be seen on this rare postcard view by Glover, there was also a spectator area and electric lighting and bunting, while refreshments were available from the pier kiosk. Roller hockey matches and horse races using basket horses were also a feature of the rink, which survived until the demise of the pier in the Second World War. A new rink was opened after the war in the Rotunda Amusement Park.

56. Donkeys were one of the best-loved features of the seaside, yet until a few years prior to the First World War they were rarely seen in Folkestone as they were regarded as a working class pleasure. This postcard dates from 1913 and is captioned 'The Burlington Donkey Derby Lower Sandgate Road Folkestone 6.30 a.m. – all members of the Burlington staff in the photo'. The Burlington was (and still is) a high-class hotel, just off the Leas in Earls Avenue, that was opened in 1893. Why there was such an early start is a mystery (perhaps they had to go to work), nevertheless the riders appear to be in blithe spirits judging by their outfits. Two of the men are dressed as women, while a third looks resplendent in his jockey's silks. Another sports a clown-like face and the other is clothed in 'coster' garb of flat cap and scarf. It would be interesting to know who won.

57. Before the First World War Folkestone, as was the case with many select seaside resorts, abounded with private schools for the children of the prosperous West End of the town. They ranged in size from just a few pupils to hundreds, with the larger schools also housing sports grounds. One such school was St. Mary's Convent off Shorncliffe Road, shown here on this postcard by F.J. Parsons just prior to the Great War during a sports day or prize giving. Due to the intense competition many of the smaller schools were short-lived, while others never reopened after the war. One of the survivors was St. Mary's Convent and it is now one of the very few private schools left in the town. In 1998 it combined with the neighbouring Dover College Junior School at Westbrook House and they became jointly known as St. Mary's Westbrook. Another option for the wealthy Edwardian Folkestonian was to engage a private tutor to teach his children at home. Many such tutors advertised their services in the local newspapers before the First World War.

58. The onset of the First World War on 4th August 1914 was to change the face of Folkestone forever. The holiday town was transformed into a front-line garrison town crammed full of Belgian refugees, soldiers rest camps and troops embarking and returning from the Western Front. Yet in spite of its military importance (the large Shorncliffe army camp was also just outside the town) Folkestone was spared German raids for three years. Many townsfolk believed it was due to the help given by Folkestone fishermen to the sailors of the *Grosser Kurfurst* that sank off the coast on 31st May 1878 with the loss of 284 lives. This illusion was cruelly shattered, however, during the early evening of Friday 25th May 1917 when 21 German Gotha bombers dropped 51 bombs on Folkestone killing 72 persons, a single bomb in Tontine Street accounting for 61 of them. This more unusual view of the raid shows the wreckage of Nos. 19 and 21 Bouverie Road East, where five people were killed.

59. The town's 413 military dead of the First World War (but sadly not its civilian) were honoured with this splendid war memorial designed by F.V. Blundstone and unveiled on Saturday, 2nd December 1922. It was sited at the top of the Slope Road to the harbour, which was renamed the Road of Remembrance after the war in honour of the many troops who trudged up and down it on their way to and from the front line. The smaller Cairn Memorial, dating from 1927, was also erected nearby with the inscription 'During the Great War, tens of thousands of British Soldiers passed along the road on their way to and from the battlefields of Europe' and these lines by Tennyson 'Not once or twice in our rough island history, the path of duty was the way to glory'. Surrounding the memorial is a bed of rosemary, the herb of remembrance. A third memorial on the Leas commemorates air force personnel who lost their lives in both world wars.

FOLKESTONE'S WAR MEMORIAL.

60. Folkestone's Royal Victoria Hospital, opened on 3rd July 1890, was understandably kept very busy during the Great War and as such its original nurses home was converted into accommodation for injured soldiers. The nurses were transferred to a temporary home at Nos. 18 and 20 St. John's Church Road, though they were to remain there until 29th July 1922 when a brand new nurses home at the hospital was opened, as featured on this postcard. HRH the Prince of Wales had laid the foundation stone to the home on 27th July 1921 and later the same year the Brotherhood of Cheerful Sparrows raised the sum of £1,245, which enabled the first part to be completed. They later raised another £1,819 and, along with a donation of £4,000, this enabled the home to be finished. Matron Browne and a group of her nurses can be seen on the left, while on the right stand a group of civic dignitaries including Sir Stephen Penfold, the Countess of Rocksavage (who formally opened the home), the Mayor R.G. Wood and Sir Philip Sassoon M.P.

THE ZIG-ZAG PATH.   FOLKESTONE. Nº 154.

61. Following the end of the First World War it soon became apparent that many of Folkestone's wealthier visitors now preferred to travel abroad or to quieter destinations for their holidays. The golden years of Fashionable Folkestone were now over and the town had to reinvent itself as a holiday resort. In keeping with its tradition as Kent's most select watering place, working-class visitors were still somewhat frowned upon (*Let them go to Margate* said one councillor), but sights were now firmly set on attracting a more middle class clientele. The Town Council now styled Folkestone as 'Floral Folkestone' and planted numerous flowerbeds around the town. To complement this new approach a number of additional attractions were provided, including the Zig-Zag Path that ran down the cliff from the Leas Bandstand to the Lower Sandgate Road. Opened in 1921, the path was designed by J.R. Pulham of Margate with a border with 'Pulhamite' Rock and flowerbeds, sheltered seating and no steps, so easing the access to the seafront for the disabled. The Zig-Zag remains an attractive feature today and has recently undergone refurbishment, including the provision of an amphitheatre at its lower entrance.

62. The last vestiges of snobbery down on the seafront had disappeared by the 1920s when this photograph was taken and middle and working class visitors were far more in evidence. The old attractions largely remained, including the Victoria Pier with its popular beauty and novelty contests and Cardow's Cadets in the Red Roof Chalet. The rows of huts included refreshment and newsagent's stalls and a motor coach booking office for trips to Margate, Rye, Hastings, Herne Bay, Canterbury and London. Beyond the stalls is the RNLI station, opened in 1893 to house the *J. McConnell Hussey* donated by Miss J. Curling of Denmark Hill, London. The boat was called out only four times in ten years before being replaced by the self-righting *Leslie* in March 1903. As we have seen the *Leslie* was quite active in its early years, but after the First World War was rarely called upon and its use was largely confined to fundraising until the station was closed in October 1930 with the *Leslie* having saved 16 lives from 27 launches.

63. One of the great characters of inter-war Folkestone was Captain Sidney Lawson Smith, who gave diving exhibitions from the Victoria Pier. This colourful individual had spent his childhood in London and during the First World War fought with the Royal Artillery until he was injured in 1915. He then became involved with the salvage section of the Royal Navy and upon resumption of peace joined the Merchant Navy where he gained a Master's Certificate. He trained as a diver in 1921 and settling in Eastbourne began his career as a lecturer in the winter and exhibition diver during the summer. A typical Lawson Smith day on the pier consisted of describing through a loudspeaker the workings of the diving equipment, and after being lowered to the seabed, explaining the mysteries of the deep. Occasionally his repertoire even extended to the rendition of old sea shanties! Upon returning to the pier, he would invite questions and sell signed postcards of himself at 6d per time. He was indeed a great showman and revelled in the fact he was once apprehended for walking on the Leas with his diving gear during a band concert, for which he was fined £1. Another time at Eastbourne, he was fined for stomping around the pier during an orchestral performance.

64. Whereas before 1914 Folkestone's seaside attractions had been promoted by private enterprise, by the 1920s the Town Council was taking the lead in providing new leisure facilities for both locals and visitors. This photograph shows the official opening day of the Marine Gardens Pavilion on 1st March 1926 after it had been erected by local builder O. Marx for the Council at a cost of £15,000. The powers to erect the building had been obtained in 1920 and its design was based on Westbrook Pavilion in Margate (destroyed in a storm in 1953). The pavilion proved to be a versatile asset over the years by hosting concert parties (particularly the much-loved 'Bouquets'), variety shows, a skating rink and events of all kinds. Live performances were discontinued after 'Showtime' was transferred to the Leas Cliff Hall in 1981 and the building has now been divided up into a café bar, pub and nightclub.

Leas Cliff Hall, Folkestone.

65. In the following year Folkestone's 'Jewel in the Crown' as regards entertainment buildings finally saw the light of day when HRH Prince Henry, Duke of Gloucester, officially opened the Leas Cliff Hall on 13th July 1927. Designed by J.L. Seaton Dahl back in 1913, work was not commenced on the site of the Leas Shelter until 1925, and this postcard shows the building nearing completion (note the workmen on the lower floor). The eventual cost of the hall was to be £80,000 and as can be seen it was laid out on three levels, each with balconies, while the flat roof at ground level was used as a sundeck. The exterior consisted of sand-faced stucco and colour washed walls below the main hall and light coloured terracotta on the upper walls. Internally the main hall measured 122 x 67 feet and was enriched with fibrous ornamentation. A useful, if never particularly profitable, addition to the town, the Leas Cliff Hall has proved its worth over the years. The building is currently leased out by Shepway District Council and has recently undergone extensive refurbishment.

66. For thirteen years from 1927 until 1940 Folkestone had its own Municipal Orchestra based at the Leas Cliff Hall and it is pictured here in 1928 with its conductor and musical director Eldridge Newman. Upon the hall's opening Captain Algernon Holland was appointed musical director of the 25-piece orchestra at a salary of £20 per month and he was contracted to provide 16 concerts per week throughout the year. However, the new hall lost money in its first year and Captain Holland, dissatisfied about a number of matters including pay, resigned in May 1928. He was replaced by 39-year-old James William Eldridge Newman, a violinist who had previously been conductor of Weymouth Municipal orchestra since 1925. Newman quickly formed a Municipal Choir of 200 and established Thursday as his symphony concert evening. He soon acquired a name for himself, which led to the BBC frequently broadcasting concerts by the orchestra. In 1930 Newman founded an annual September music festival when the orchestra was augmented to 60, yet financial constrictions meant that by 1939 it had been reduced to just an octet with Newman now a playing member. The orchestra was disbanded early during the Second World War and in May 1940 Newman joined the Buffs, yet sadly he was soon to meet a most mysterious end when he was found shot dead on 15th November 1940 in a park outside Maidstone. The coroner's verdict was 'suicide, balance of mind disturbed' (others maintained Newman was murdered), yet he was still given a military funeral at Shorncliffe Military Cemetery.

1057 – KINGSNORTH GARDENS FOLKESTONE. Wiseman Homer

67. In their bid to promote Floral Folkestone, the Town Council's Parks Superintendent G.E. Roden laid out Kingsnorth Gardens in a clay pit near the Central Station. The gardens, named in honour of John Kingsnorth who had used the pit for brick making, cost £3,500 in total and were officially opened by Lord and Lady Radnor on 27th June 1928. This postcard by Wiseman Homer shows the gardens soon after opening with the tower of the United Reform Church in the distance. As well as thousands of shrubs and plants, and the pergola featured in this picture, the gardens contained two large ponds with fountains, smaller ponds, lawns, statues of Pan and Sir Jeffrey Hudson (Court Dwarf to Charles I) and sheltered paths and seating. Shepway District Council, to their credit, keep the gardens immaculate and they are a very popular rendezvous for both townsfolk and students from the nearby South Kent College.

68. If donkey rides were not a particular feature of Folkestone, then rides behind a llama were during the 1920s and 1930s! The Rodwell family operated these 'South American Camels' as they were known and a ride cost 1s. This postcard by Seaman's Studio from 1928 shows one of the llamas on the Leas passing the Harvey Statue erected in honour of Folkestone's most famous son William Harvey. Harvey, the son of a prominent townsman who was four times Mayor, was born on 1st April 1578 in a house off Mercery Lane (now Church Street). He was educated at King's School, Canterbury and Cambridge University and studied under the eminent physician Fabricius at Padua, Italy, where he gained his doctorate in 1602. Elected to the Royal College of Physicians in 1604, Harvey was appointed physician to St. Bartholomew's Hospital in 1609, which in turn led him in 1618 to be selected as Court Physician to James I (and later Charles I). His pioneering work on the circulation of blood (for which he is chiefly remembered) *Anatomical Experiments in the Action of the Heart and Blood* was published in 1628. Harvey died in 1657 and his will left £200 to the poor of Folkestone. Part of this money was used to found a free school, which opened in 1674 and continues to flourish as the Harvey Grammar School. His commemorative bronze statue by Albert Joy was unveiled in 1881 and every year on the 1st April is the scene of a wreath-laying ceremony by members of the medical profession.

69. Down in the fishmarket area, the 1930s would finally bring about the long-planned for redevelopment first proposed in 1913 (see photograph 46). The Town Council took this photograph of Radnor Street in 1928 when the earlier demolition scheme was reconfirmed. Radnor Street, originally known as Fishermen's Row, ran just behind the Stade and indeed the three pubs seen (the Jubilee, Ship and Oddfellows Arms) had entrances in both thoroughfares. By now, however, there was some opposition to the proposals, claiming the character of the area would be ruined, yet demolition commenced in April 1935 after 34 families were moved to the new Canterbury Road Estate. The three pubs were rebuilt on the Stade, leaving the new Radnor Street to become an insignificant access road to the fishmarket. The destruction of Great and Little Fenchurch Streets was to follow in 1937 as the Council continued its intensive council house building programme started in the 1920s. In 1934 the Borough of Folkestone had been expanded to include Cheriton and Sandgate and in 1936 the population of the town stood at around 40,000.

70. By the 1930s Sandgate Road was beginning to supplant Tontine Street as Folkestone's main shopping street and this was confirmed with the opening of Bobby's new department store. Bobby's had transferred from Rendezvous Street (where they had been established since 1906) to their new purpose-built premises, complete with ornate canopy, on 6th March 1931, and within a few years they had extended into the adjoining building previously occupied by Lewis & Hyland. Eventually in 1972, Bobby's became Debenhams, which remains Folkestone's leading department store. This Valentine's postcard from 1936 also shows the Esplanade Hotel on the right, which had opened as the Bates Hotel in 1859 and was a popular hostelry with locals until its demolition in 1972. This section of Sandgate Road was converted into a pedestrian precinct in 1984.

THE NEW UNDERCLIFF WALK. FOLKESTONE 20

71. The various harbour works over the years had led to a covering of sand building up below the East Cliff and after Lord Radnor had given the area to the town in 1924 it was developed as a second beach and leisure area for Folkestone. The old SER workshops, closed in 1922, were acquired by the Town Council in 1927 for £3,200 and converted into bathing cabins, while the new undercliff walk seen here was built below the cliff giving access to the beach, which had been cleared of rocks. This postcard by the Norman Series shows the promenade in about 1930, before it was replaced by the present Coronation Parade in 1935. The bathing cabins (out of picture to the left) were removed in 1960 to make way for the Sunny Sands restaurant, which in turn was demolished in the 1980s for a block of flats. A section of the beach was utilised for a new pumping station for Southern Water in 2000, which includes a terrace café.

Boating Pool and Amusement Rotunda, Folkestone. 2813.

74. The area adjoining the open-air swimming pool was developed as an amusement park; the first leaseholder being Fred Harrison who previously kept his amusements on the Victoria Pier. This postcard by Shoesmith & Etheridge shows the boating pool and Rotunda amusement dome shortly after they were constructed in 1937 and 1938 respectively. In 1955 the lease of the park passed to John Cooper, and then in 1973 to Jimmy Godden. He purchased the freehold of the area in 1981 and the boating pool disappeared to make way for more rides. The Rotunda was joined by a sister structure from Holland in 1984, but was demolished in December 2002 when a large part of the amusement park was sold to Trent Developments, whose plans for the site include a multiplex cinema, ten pin bowling centre, supermarket, underground carpark and housing.

75. If the First World War changed the resort character of Folkestone, then the Second World War dealt it a mighty blow from which it has never fully recovered. Situated in what was christened 'Hellfire Corner' the town was badly savaged by German bombing and shelling that killed at least 86 recorded civilians. The heart of old Folkestone around the Inner Harbour was destroyed by a parachute mine on 18th November 1940 and this photograph from the late 1940s shows some of the few buildings in the area that survived; albeit in a damaged state. They include the Wellington and Chequers public houses on the left, while beyond the Chequers can be viewed the fenced off cellar of the South Foreland public house seen in photograph 52. All these buildings would soon be pulled down, to be replaced by car parks and general emptiness – the distinctive charm of the area being lost forever. Worse was to follow as from the 1960s Folkestone, in common with many resorts, began to seriously decline as a holiday centre. As a result many of its larger hotels and visitor facilities ceased to function and in some cases were demolished.

FOLKESTONE

76. Yet let us not end on a low, but on this recent multi-view postcard courtesy of J. Salmon, which shows some of the attractions Folkestone (now part of Shepway District Council and boasting a population of around 49,000) still has to offer. The top left-hand picture shows the harbour, while in the centre is the lower station of the Leas Lift, the second oldest water-balance lift in the country. The Leas seen in the top right-hand picture is still one of England's best cliff-top promenades and its western end in particular still evokes a sense of a once grand past. The Warren in the lower left-hand picture remains a rambler's paradise and a haven of tranquillity. The lower right-hand picture looks across the harbour to the Grand Burstin Hotel. The Burstin may not be everyone's cup of tea architecturally, yet there's no denying it is a very successful short break hotel that brings many visitors into the town. New attractions have included the Lower Leas Coastal Park, and in 2002 a Russian Submarine and land train. With plans for a new marina development at the harbour in the offing, some of these views themselves may soon become history.